TODDLER
&Teddy

BayBooks
An imprint of HarperCollins*Publishers*

A Bay Books Publication
An imprint of HarperCollinsPublishers

First published in Australia in 1992 by Bay Books, of
CollinsAngus&Robertson Publishers Pty Limited (ACN 009 913 517)
A division of HarperCollinsPublishers (Australia) Pty Limited
25-31 Ryde Road, Pymble NSW 2073, Australia

HarperCollinsPublishers (New Zealand) Limited
31 View Road, Glenfield, Auckland 10, New Zealand

HarperCollinsPublishers Limited
77-85 Fulham Palace Road, London W6 8JB, United Kingdom

National Library of Australia
Cataloguing-in-Publication data:

Kate Tully.
    Toddler & Teddy/Spring and Summer.

    ISBN 1 86378 012 2

    1. Needlework – Patterns. 2. Children's clothing.
    3. Children's rooms. I. Pereira, Sally. II. Title.
    (Series: Bay Books craft collection)

746.4

Project Manager: Kate Tully
Fashion Editor: Sally Pereira
Photographer: Andrew Elton
Stylist: Louise Wilkinson
Knitting Consultant: Sheryl Braden

Special thanks to the models: Elizabeth, James,
Oliver, Patrick, Peta, Robert, Sam and Shannon

Printed in Singapore

5 4 3 2 1
96 95 94 93 92

Contents

Introduction

Toddler & Teddy (Spring/Summer) is the first edition in an ongoing series of original, appealing, fun and practical books. This edition presents a bounty of great things to make for special little people. There are literally dozens of designs for clothes for one to four-year-olds, plus twenty projects for their bedrooms.

There is a full size pattern sheet and simple, comprehensive instructions for every project, to make it easy to create the season's most delightful clothes and rooms.

The clothes included in this edition are fashionable and fun to wear, and are bound to become your toddler's favourites. Projects such as the stencilled playmat and chalkboard, among others, will provide many hours of enjoyment and your toddler will really love going to bed in a new set of tartan pyjamas under an appliquéd doona cover.

These and many more will endear you to the lucky toddler who gets them!. Whatever projects you choose to make, have fun and enjoy yourself. Before you know it you won't want to stop and you'll have the trendiest toddler in town!

Dream upon a star

S tars are a magical motif for children's rooms, helping to create a mystical, dreamy atmosphere which fuels their already vivid imaginations. In this room, stars have been combined with the alphabet to remind us that children are embarking on a lifetime of learning, and with monograms to say that here is a sanctuary created just for this child.

An alphabet in the colours of spring flowers has been translated with equal effect into stencilling and cross stitch to achieve a look which is completely integrated yet offers an appealing variety in textures. And stars pop up everywhere, just like they do on a summer's night.

In this chapter, you'll learn how to stencil the wall frieze and curtains as well as embellish accessories like the lampshade, shelf, box and blocks. And you'll see how, with some time and dedication, you can create a beautiful heirloom birth sampler and throw rug, plus smaller cross stitch projects like the towel and sheet trims and personalised bibs.

All the help you need is in the instructions starting on page 48, and the special Stencilling Tips on page 49.

"Stars lay like yellow pollen that from a flower has fallen ..."

ANDREW JOHN YOUNG

Acknowledgements: All cross-stitching designed and stitched by Jane West. Stencilling designed and executed by Louise Wilkinson. Additional sewing by Libby Wilkinson. Craft materials from DMC/Myart. Fabrics and trims from Lincraft. Teddies from Teddy & Friends. Framing by Framing Corner, Chatswood, NSW. Clock and photo frame from Bonza Brats. Ambi bird and rattle from Hide 'n' Seek. Blanket and cup from Hartland Fashion Agencies. Toiletries from The Body Shop. Flowers from Sweet Violets. Towels by Sheridan. Blind by Luxaflex. Furniture from Grace Bros. Lamp from Task Lighting/Freedom Furniture. Paint below frieze is Moody Blue by Dulux. Stockist details on page 78.

STENCILLED FRIEZE
(Instructions page 48)

A stencilled frieze is a simple but effective
way to decorate the walls of baby's room
— it's more fun than wall-papering and not
nearly as messy! It forms a perfect
background to all the other bits and pieces
that will fill the room with fun and colour.

STENCILLED CURTAINS & LAMPSHADE

(Instructions pages 48–49)

Transform plain curtains with a stencilled alphabet and ribbon trim. Stencil some stars on a lampshade for a well-lit starry night.

STENCILLED SHELF

(Instructions page 49)

A stencilled shelf can come in handy for all sorts of babys' odds and ends — store mugs, toothbrush, baby's special toy and anything at all that needs its very own place.

"... continuous as the stars that shine and twinkle on the milky way ..."

WILLIAM WORDSWORTH

STENCILLED BOX
(Instructions page 49)

Put toys, teddies and towels in a star-stencilled wooden box for easy access and safe-keeping. Experiment with various colour combinations to suit your baby's room and décor. You might even want to make a box for your own bits and pieces.

STENCILLED BLOCKS , CROSS STITCH BIB
(Instructions pages 49, 60)

What better than a personalised bib for baby to make his or her very own mess on. And these blocks with stencilled letters and stars can be a colourful addition to the toy box — use as many varied colours as you fancy.

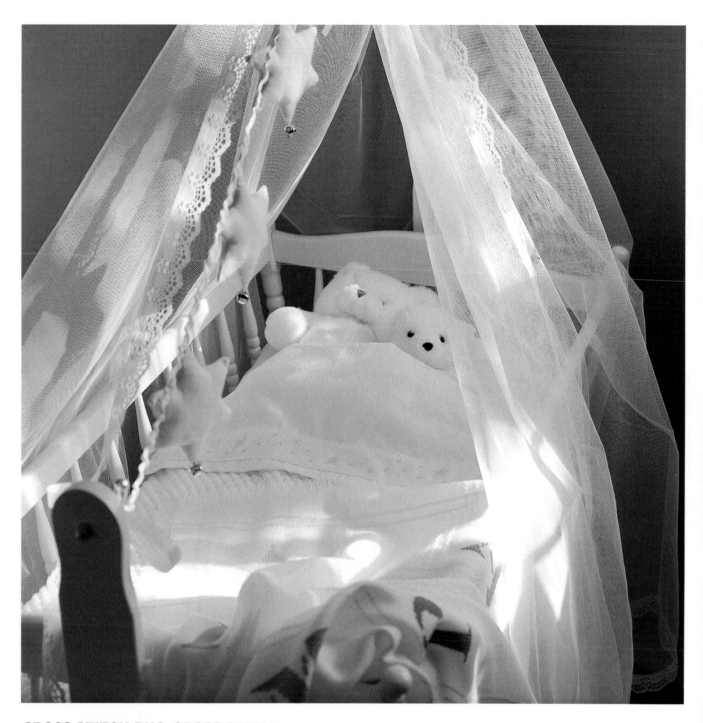

**CROSS STITCH RUG, CROSS STITCH
SHEET TRIM, CRIB STARS**
(Instructions pages 60, 53, 53)

Baby will really 'dream upon a star' to the sound
of bells on these crib stars, and under a cross
stitched sheet and rug for a warm, cosy and
peaceful night's sleep.

CROSS STITCH SAMPLER
(Instructions page 60)

A cross-stitched sampler makes an ideal decoration for the baby's room, with the name and birthdate of the baby too. Make sure you consult with a picture framer before mounting the work, to ensure the best possible result.

Tops & tails

*Roses are red,
violets
are blue,
tops & tails
are too good
to be true*

Take a very simple shorts pattern and a purchased t-shirt, and let your imagination transform them into outfits which are destined to become favourites. These projects need only basic skills and materials, and the results are terrific!

These tops and tails use an inexpensive purchased t-shirt and a simple shorts pattern. For instructions, turn to page 61.

In this section you will find t-shirt and short combinations which involve all sorts of handiwork. There's the t-shirt with teddy appliqué and a charming outfit with tartan bowtie. The gingham shorts with t-shirt rimmed to match is lovely in pink as shown but use any colour you fancy. As for the patchwork shirt and shorts outfit, there is no limit to the creations you can put together. Piece together all sorts of fashions for your toddler. Don't forget to refer to the Machine Appliqué Tips on page 74 — but after a couple of 'tops and tails' outfits you'll be an expert and your toddler will feel tops!

Acknowledgements: All garments designed and made by Sally Pereira. 'Sigmund' teddy from Teddy & Friends. Fabrics from Hill Textiles and Ray Toby. Trims from Heritage Trims. Paint is 'Fashion Show' Shiny Dimensional Fabric Paint from Myart. T-shirts from a leading chain store. Stockist details on page 78.

TOPS & TAILS

(Use the shorts pattern on page 61, then use the ideas on pages 16–19 to make terrific outfits)

TEDDY AT THE READY

This appliqué teddy is dressed up and ready for fun. Cut him out using three fabrics and the outline on page 61, then appliqué onto t-shirt. (See Machine Appliqué Tips, on page 74).
The striped waistcoat fabric is also used for the shorts.

DAPPER

A striped cotton knit makes smart shorts and matching bib, set off by a dapper bowtie and coordinating buttons. Cut a bib pattern by tracing around neckedge and armhole seams, then adding scoop. Cut out bib and appliqué to the t-shirt. (See Machine Appliqué Tips on page 74). Cut four circles from tartan ribbon and appliqué onto bib. Make bow tie from tartan ribbon and stitch into place.

PRETTY IN PINK

Pretty broderie anglaise trims dress up this pink t-shirt and shorts. The ready-gathered broderie is stitched to the braid and tied with a pink satin ribbon. It is then attached to the t-shirt by press studs at centre front and back, so that it comes off for washing. The pink gingham shorts are trimmed in the same braid.

ALL PATCHED UP

Purchased patches are a quick, easy and effective way to add lots of interest. These are simply stitched to the t-shirt and lightweight denim shorts, which are top-stitched in a deeper colour.

PIECING IT TOGETHER

Colour blocking is easy and eye-catching. Cut the t-shirt off under the arms and add bands of contrasting colour, finishing with the bottom of the t-shirt sewn back into place. Divide each side of the shorts halfway along the leg and make up in separate colours. Topstitching adds a neat finish.

PICTURE THIS

The design of the braid trim on the shorts has been copied onto the t-shirt using dimensional fabric paint. Very coordinated! The shorts have a patch pocket also trimmed with the braid.

APPLIED ART

Motifs from the print of
these colourful shorts
have been individually
cut out and appliquéd
onto a coloured t-shirt.
See Machine Appliqué
Tips on page 74.

CHECK THIS OUT

Noughts and crosses
games make the perfect
complement to these
smart tartan shorts.
The games are applied
with dimensional fabric
paints, taking the cue
for their colours from
the many colours of
the shorts.

Let's go boating

Navy blue plus red and white. A combination that never fails to look fresh and smart, evoking images of sunny days 'messing about in boats'.

Take those three trusty colours, dress them up with some well-used spots and stripes and add a traditional sailor's collar, and you have this stylish collection of clothes for boys and girls.

There are practical, easy-care knits in tops, bottoms and a very cute little dress, plus crisp cotton shorts and pants. For the finishing touch, there's also the oh-so-smart wide-brimmed hat that no fashion-conscious toddler can do without!

Everything you need to know to create this marvellous, coordinated summer wardrobe is contained in the instructions starting on page 62. And don't miss Stretch Knit Tips on page 63.

"Come sail with me across the sea ..."

Acknowledgements: All garments designed and made by Sally Pereira, except for Anchor Knit Top designed by Sheryl Braden. Fabrics from Hill Textiles and Ray Toby. Trims from Lincraft. Tote bag from McCalls pattern 5356. Teddies from Teddy & Friends. Shoes and socks from Bonza Brats. Scarves and braces from Hartland Fashion Agencies. Toys from Hide 'n' Seek.

CROPPED RAGLAN TOP & SKIRT
(Instructions pages 62–63)

A summer sailor's outfit — a cropped raglan top with a skirt is perfect for a summer day. Forget about keeping her top tucked in!

RAGLAN TOP & PANEL PANTS
(Instructions pages 62–63)

An irresistible and well-dressed sailor — team a long-sleeved raglan top with panel pants and a hat for a bright and never-out-of-fashion combination. And don't forget to buy some boating shoes to complete the outfit.

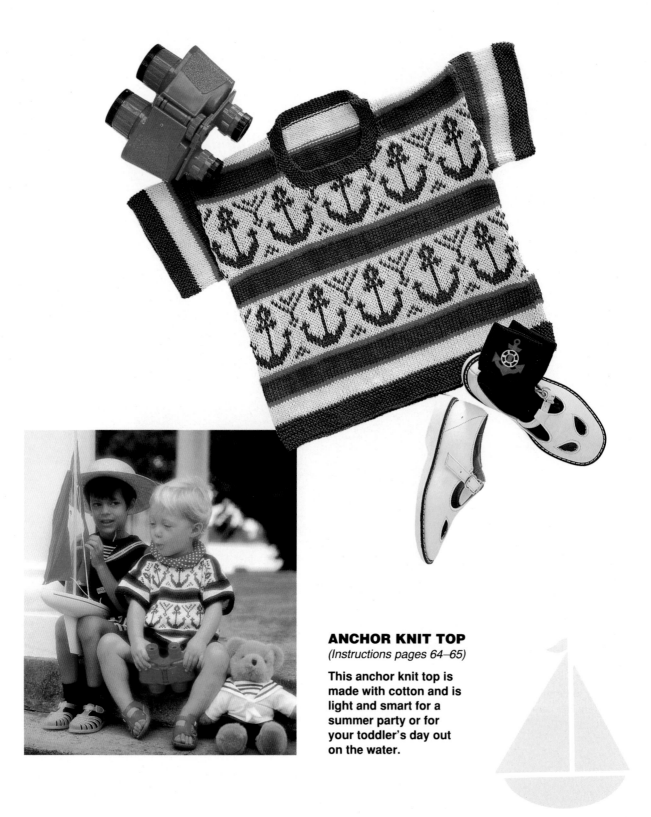

ANCHOR KNIT TOP
(Instructions pages 64–65)

This anchor knit top is made with cotton and is light and smart for a summer party or for your toddler's day out on the water.

SAILOR TOP & PANEL SHORTS
(Instructions pages 63)

Too good to be true — a true blue Aussie sailor! A perfect suit for boys and girls — sailor top with striped inset and ribbon trim, and striped panel shorts. Simple to make and simply so suitable for summer and spring!

SAILOR DRESS
(Instructions page 64)

Dressed to impress in blue and white spots and stripes. So versatile for both casual and smart occasions, this dress is bound to become a favourite in the wardrobe.

PANEL & STRIPED HATS
(Instructions page 64)

Top off your toddler's new nautical outfit with a smart panelled or striped hat, essential for protection on those hot summer days. Make one for toddler's teddy too!

Home sweet home

The charm of patchwork is evergreen, especially when it combines those well-loved motifs, the heart and the home. This room gives a friendly country-style welcome, making your toddler feel comfortably at home with elements that are as practical as they are colourful.

When it comes to choosing fabrics that have the same lasting appeal as patchwork, it's hard to go past tartans. Two different tartans are combined here with a range of other fabrics against a background of white for a clean, simple, irresistible country effect.

The projects in this chapter take traditional patchwork designs then make them even easier to appliqué and stencil, using modern techniques. (Stencilling Tips on page 49 and Machine Appliqué Tips on page 74 show how to achieve a truly professional finish).

Make a gorgeous yet practical removable quilt cover with matching pillowslip and large cushions. Create a unique, wipe-clean stencilled playmat, plus coordinated chalkboard and experiment with a variety of other simple craft ideas to stretch your imagination. Instructions for this section start on page 66.

"Home is where the heart is"

PROVERB

Acknowledgements: Patchwork and appliqué by Libby Wilkinson. Stencilling by Louise Wilkinson. Additional sewing by Helen Murphy. Fabrics from Ray Toby. Craft materials from DMC/Myart. Teddies from Teddy & Friends. Box kits from Lincraft. Teddy cart, sign and teddy on bicycle from Brosalco. Beret and shoes from Hartland Fashion Agencies. Bookends and fire engine music box from Hide 'n' Seek.

29

STENCILLED PLAYMAT
(Instructions page 66)

Playful toddlers can eat and drink on this stencilled mat and make as much mess as they like and it will all wipe clean.

STENCILLED CHALKBOARD
(Instructions page 66)

Encourage inquisitive toddlers to the chalkboard with some colourful stencilled designs. A pinboard will show off some of their favourite cards and photos.

"Home, home, sweet, sweet home!
There's no place like home, there's no place like home!"

JOHN HOWARD PAYNE

DOONA COVER & PILLOW SLIP

(Instructions pages 67–68)

Toddler and teddy can dream the night away under a tartan-trimmed and appliquéd doona cover with pillow slip to match. Perhaps toddler can show teddy how to read!

**HEART CUSHION
WITH BOWS**
(Instructions page 67)

**Home is where the heart
is and this heart cushion
with bows is a terrific
addition to the toddler's
home.**

CURTAIN SASHES
(Instructions page 68)

**Tartan sashes add a
finishing touch to a
room filled with country
colours and fun things
to look at and play with.**

PYJAMAS
(Instructions page 71)

**Two terrible toddlers
in tartan pyjamas look
terribly smart.**

NEEDLEPOINT KEEPSAKE HOUSE
(Instructions pages 71–72)

Teddy certainly likes this needlepoint house and toddler surely will too.

TODDLER & TEDDY

Fun in the sun

Sunny days at the beach are a delight for toddlers, with opportunities to explore the sand and water, paddle in rock pools and chase tiny fish.

A toddler's beach wardrobeshould be flexible enough to cope with the varying range of temperatures during a typical day in the sun. That task is made as simple as can be with the fun clothes to make in this chapter.

There is delightful swimwear for both boys and girls, teamed with stylish tops and bottoms in various lengths, from a crop top and shorts to a full hooded tracksuit to provide plenty of protection from wind and the falling temperatures of late afternoon.

The whole collection has been made in those favourite fabrics, stretch cotton knits. Easy to sew, easy to care for and easy to wear.

The colour range reflects the tones of coral and exotic fish, and most of the garments are trimmed with specially designed appliqué fish and starfish to give a unique finish. If you've never tried this type of sewing before, you will see how easy it is to create professional-looking appliqué with our Machine Appliqué Tips on page 74. Turn to the instructions on page 73 for this section.

"Sing me a song, a good song of the sea ..."

TRADITIONAL

Acknowledgements: All garments designed and made by Sally Pereira, except Fish and Starfish Knit Top designed by Sheryl Braden. Fabrics from Hill Textiles. Teddies from Teddy & Friends. Shoes and sunglasses from Bonza Brats. Headband from Hartland Fashion Agencies. Fish from Hide 'n' Seek. Deck lounge from The Teddy Bear Shop. Blinker sunglasses from The Cancer Council of NSW.

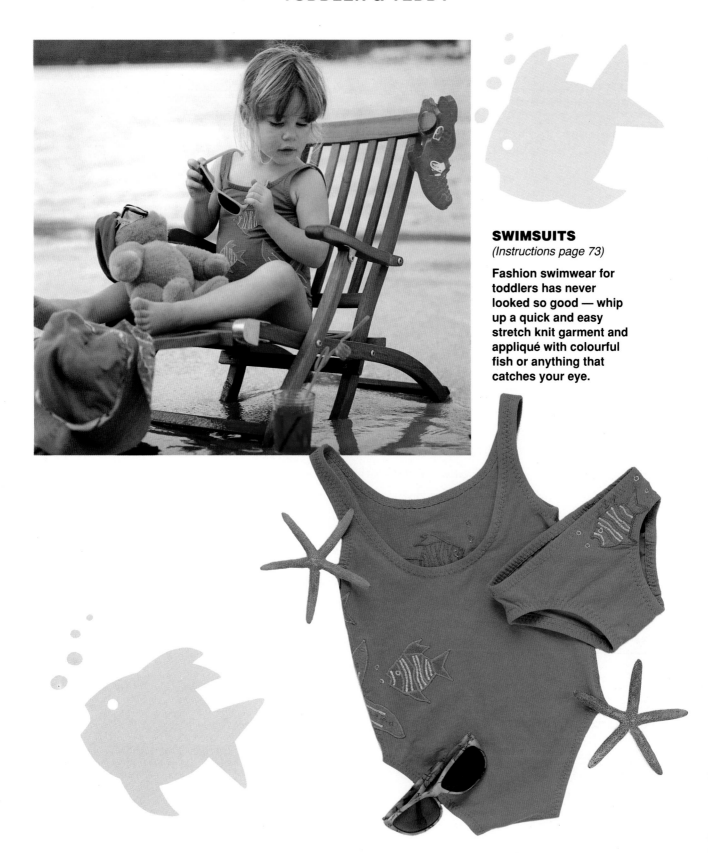

SWIMSUITS
(Instructions page 73)

Fashion swimwear for toddlers has never looked so good — whip up a quick and easy stretch knit garment and appliqué with colourful fish or anything that catches your eye.

T-SHIRT & SHORTS
(Instructions page 74)

**All toddlers have
t-shirts and shorts in
their summer wardrobe
but these will stand out
from the crowd.**

TRACK PANTS & HOODED TRACK TOP
(Instructions page 75)

Long summer days can become cool summer evenings and a stretch knit track suit is just the thing to wrap up your toddler. It's also light enough to wear during the day as protection from the sun.

"Everyone loves to play in the sun and feel the sand between their toes"

CROP TOP & PIRATE PANTS
(Instructions page 74)

A crop top and pirate pants are perfect for a bit of a breeze on a steamy day.

FISH & STARFISH KNIT TOP
(Instructions pages 76–77)

This cotton knit top, embroidered with fish and starfish looks so cool and comfortable.

WIDE-BRIMMED HAT
(Instructions page 73)

An essential thing to take to the beach — top your
toddler's head with a colourful wide-brimmed hat or
appliqué a bright peak cap for a totally sun-safe day.
Don't forget to take the blockout too.

Down to detail

Using the pattern sheet

The instructions for each garment indicate the numbers of the pattern pieces required. Pattern pieces for all garments appear full-size on the pull-out pattern sheet at the back of the book. There are two size patterns for each garment, as indicated in the instructions. All pattern pieces for each size (1, 2, 3 and 4) are shown on the pattern sheet in the same type of line (e.g. solid or dotted). The size of each pattern piece is also indicated on the piece, alongside the piece number.

1 Make a note of the numbers of required pattern pieces from the instructions. Find each number in the top or bottom margin of the pattern sheet, then run your finger down or up the sheet until you find the pattern piece in the size you want. Highlight the piece with a felt-tip highlighting pen.

2 When all the pieces have been highlighted, place the pattern sheet on a hard, flat surface and secure with masking tape. Secure a piece of ordinary tracing paper (from a newsagent or haberdasher) over the highlighted pieces and trace them. Write the pattern piece number and size on the traced piece, and remember to also transfer grainline and other markings and instructions. If there

is a garment you think you will make many times, it is worth tracing the pattern onto non-woven interfacing which will last longer than paper.

3 Adjust patterns if necessary, referring to the size chart here.

4 Before cutting fabric, place all pattern pieces to check layout, making sure that stripes or prints all run in the same direction. Allow also for simple pieces such as neckbands or skirts for which there is no pattern piece but whose dimensions are given in the instructions. Cut out all pieces (seam allowances are included).

5 When you have finished with your traced pattern pieces, fold them and put them into the pattern envelope (see instructions on page 79).

Patterns for all other projects accompany the instructions in the book.

Sizes

All clothes are cut generously to be comfortable for most children aged 1 to 4. When choosing the correct pattern size for children's clothes, the height of the child is the determining factor.

Check your child's measurements against this chart. Length can be easily altered by lengthening or shortening pattern pieces prior to cutting. Correct fitting is especially important for the swimwear.

Seams

Unless otherwise stated: seam allowances are 1 cm throughout, hem allowances 3 cm, fabric requirements are for fabrics 115 cm wide, and all pieces should be joined with right sides together.

Exposed raw edges on woven fabrics should be neatened by overlock stitching, zigzag stitch or pinking shears. Raw edges of ribbing can unravel and should be neatened by overlock stitching or zigzag. Raw edges of other knit fabrics can be left raw as they will not fray. All pattern pieces are found on the pull-out pattern sheet at the back of the book. All garments have been made on a Pfaff creative sewing machine.

For further information, see Stretch Knit Tips on page 63 and Machine Appliqué Tips on page 74.

Edgestitching is done 2 mm from edge of fabric. Topstitching is done close to the pressed edge of a turned hem. For both types of stitching, use markings on presser foot to make even sewing easy.

SEWN GARMENTS				
Size	Height	Chest	Waist	Hip
1	86	52	50	56
2	92	54	51	58
3	98	56	52	60
4	104	58	53	62

All measurements given in centimetres.

Knitting abbreviations

k=knit; p=purl, st(s)=stitch(es); alt=alternate; beg=beginning; inc=increase; dec=decrease; fin=finish; fol=following; rep=repeat; patt=pattern; yn fwd=yarn forward; tbl=through back of loop; tog=together; rem=remaining; g st=garter stitch; rep=repeat; st st=stocking stitch; rs=right side row; ws=wrong side row

Knitting yarns

Quantities given are approximate as the amount of yarn in a ball varies depending on the material it is made from, as well as its finish and texture. So a 50 g ball of 8 ply will vary between brands. Make sure the shop has plenty of the colour yarn you require for a pattern.

Tension

Always check your tension and adjust it by using larger or smaller needles if necessary. Tension details are given at the beginning of the knitting patterns and these tell you the number of stitches you should have in a given measurement. If the tension is not correct, then the garment will not be the right size.

KNITWEAR

Size	Actual Chest Measurement	Length to Back Neck
1	51	25
2	57	29
3	63	32
4	69	36

All measurements given in centimetres.

Cross stitch

Cross stitch designs are worked from a chart. Each square represents one stitch. Numbers or symbols are used to represent colours.

Cross stitch should be worked from left to right and when possible, should start at the top of the design. If it is a large design, work from centre down and then turn chart and fabric and work down.

To prevent the thread from twisting, turn the needle occasionally. Before starting, put the required number of strands together by pulling out one strand at a time from skein.

When starting, leave the thread twice as long as the length of the needle on the wrong side. After embroidering, weave the thread end into 2 to 3 cm stitches on the wrong side and clip off the excess thread. When you use various kinds of coloured threads, weave and clip off any excess thread every time new thread is used.

Thread the needle with the correct amount of strands, according to the chart. Do not make a knot at the end of the thread, because it will create a bumpy surface and the project will not lie flat.

Begin by bringing your needle up from the back of the fabric at the lower left corner of the centre square. Leave at least 2.5 cm of thread extended on the back side. Hold this thread so it will be overcast as you stitch. After the thread is secured, cut away excess thread.

Continue by bringing your needle down through the upper right corner. Finish your row, then bring the needle up through the lower right corner. Cross over your previous stitch, coming down through the upper left corner.

Secure your thread by weaving it through several stitches on the back side of the project. Remember: To keep a smooth surface, do not make knots when finishing threads.

Cross stitch hints:
• When working a colour in a closely scattered area, carry the thread over rather than cutting the thread each time. It is also a good idea to use a different needle for each colour and keep the threads not in use at the front of the embroidery, not at the back where they can get tangled.
• If carrying the thread more than 1 cm, weave it through a few stitches on the wrong side. To prevent a shadow, do not carry thread across unworked areas.
• Keep the back of the project smooth and neat to avoid bumps from thread ends on the right side of the design.

Finishing: If needed, a project can be washed. Use warm water and a mild detergent. Gently squeeze the project in the detergent solution. Rinse in warm water then roll in a dry towel to abosrb water. Lay project flat to partially dry. To press project, place down on ironing surface padded with a towel. Dampen the project if it is dry. Lightly press using a moderately hot dry iron.

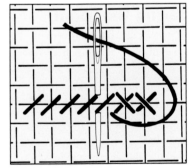

Basic cross stitch

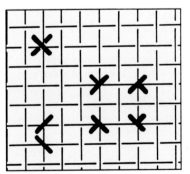

Cross stitch can also be worked as half and three-quarter stitches

DREAM UPON A STAR
Instructions

STENCILLED FRIEZE

Materials

FolkArt acrylic stencil paints:
   Apricot Cream 911
   Spring Rose 767
   Buttercup 905
   Heather 933
   Lavender Sachet 625
   Porcelain Blue 765
   Poetry Green 619
   White
Stencilling brush
Tape
Thick transparent or translucent
  plastic (stencil plastic, shirtbox
  plastic or Mylar)
Scalpel and No. 11 blade
Ruler, preferably steel
Cutting mat or thick cardboard
Indelible ink pen
Tape measure
String
Drawing pins
Tailor's chalk
Grosgrain ribbon, 1.5 cm wide x
  twice the total length of frieze
Craft glue
Saucer for paint
Dropcloths

Instructions

(Also see Stencilling Tips opposite).

Preparing the stencil

1 Photocopy the alphabet provided on pages 50 to 52.

2 Cut plastic into strips 10 cm wide. Tape a section of alphabet onto cutting mat and position plastic strip over it, centring alphabet with 2.5 cm top and bottom. Tape plastic into position.

3 Carefully cut out each letter, using scalpel and steel ruler.

4 Position separate plastic strip over a star (only one star stencil is required). Cut star in centre of plastic. Using indelible pen, draw lines 1 cm to the left and right of star across full width of plastic strip.

Preparing the room

1 Decide on height for the frieze. In each corner of room, measure from floor to desired height for middle of lower ribbon, then mark with drawing pins. Run taut string between pins.

2 Repeat 10 cm higher to mark middle of upper ribbon.

3 If desired, paint between strings in white or other background colour (white maximises stencil effect). Allow to dry completely.

Stencilling

1 Start in a corner. Squeeze paint onto saucer (each letter uses paint equal in volume to a green pea). Place stencil strip on lower string line. Dip brush into paint and wipe off excess. Holding stencil taut, dab brush over whole letter. Remove stencil.

2 Position star stencil between string lines to right of letter; space so that left hand pen line touches very edge of letter. Stencil star. Before removing stencil, mark top and bottom of right hand pen line with tailor's chalk to indicate where next letter starts.

3 Continue stencilling alternate letters and stars along complete length of frieze.

4 Remove drawing pins and string. Erase chalk marks.

5 Apply glue to end of ribbon, press into position and hold with drawing pin. Glue a length of ribbon and press onto frieze, using a long ruler to help keep it straight. This job is easiest done with two people.

STENCILLED CURTAINS

Materials

  Stencils cut for frieze
  FolkArt stencil paints as specified
   for frieze
  Stencilling brush
  Saucer for paint
  Plenty of clean scrap paper
  Pins or tape
  Grosgrain ribbon – 1.5 cm wide x
   twice width of curtain
  Continuous sheer curtaining –
   required drop x at least 1.5 times
   width of window

Instructions

1 Place wad of scrap paper on work surface. We recommend newspaper with a sheet of clean, plain paper over the top. Lay bottom of curtain over paper and pin or tape taut.

2 Using bottom of curtain as your guideline, stencil alternating letters and stars, according to instructions above.

When you have stencilled across full width of scrap paper, lift curtain, change paper and pin or tape new section of curtain over clean paper. Continue across whole curtain.

3 Pin ribbon along top and bottom of alphabet. Stitch into place.

STENCILLED SHELF
Materials
Stencils cut for frieze
FolkArt stencil paints:
  Buttercup 905
  Lavender Sachet 625
Stencilling brush
Saucer for paint
FolkArt Color aerosol basecoat:
  Poetry Green 12130
FolkArt PearlCote pearl glaze
Myart wooden shelf unit No. 07803

Instructions
1 Spray shelf with basecoat, allow to dry.
2 Stencil initial and stars.
3 Spray with pearl glaze and allow to dry 24 hours before handling.

STENCILLED LAMPSHADE
Materials
Star stencil cut for frieze
FolkArt stencil paint -
  Buttercup 905
Stencilling brush
Saucer for paint
FolkArt Color aerosol basecoat:
  Poetry Green 12130
FolkArt PearlCote pearl glaze
Plain lampshade

Instructions
1 Spray shade with basecoat and allow to dry.
2 Stencil stars around bottom edge of shade.
3 Spray with pearl glaze and allow to dry 24 hours before handling.

STENCILLING TIPS

Collecting the right equipment before you start makes the job easier and the results more pleasing.

When cutting the stencil, a fine-pointed scalpel blade is easier to manoeuvre around the details than flat-bladed cutters.

It is worth buying specially-formulated stencil paints as they dry very quickly, allowing you to move the stencil along the project at a good working pace without fear of smudging. Likewise, a proper stencilling brush has short bristles which do not retain paint like sponges.

If the edges of your stencilled motif do smudge, you are using too much paint on your brush. It is best to experiment with the technique for a few minutes before starting on a project, to get the hang of how much paint gives a complete covering without smudging.

When paint builds up on the stencil, clean with methylated spirits and allow to dry completely.

STENCILLED BOX
Materials
Star stencil cut for frieze
FolkArt stencil paint :
  Buttercup 905
Stencilling brush
Saucer for paint
FolkArt Color aerosol basecoat :
  Poetry Green 12130
FolkArt PearlCote pearl glaze
Wooden box

Instructions
1 Spray base and lid with basecoat and allow to dry.
2 Stencil stars around lid.
3 Spray base and lid with pearl glaze and allow to dry 24 hours before handling.

STENCILLED BLOCKS
Materials
Stencils cut for frieze
FolkArt stencil paints as specified for frieze
Stencilling brush
Saucer for paint
Patches of coloured fabric 12 x 12 cm, six per block
Pins
Soft filling

Instructions
1 Stencil four letter and two star patches per block.
2 With right sides facing, stitch four letter patches together to form sides of cube. Pin a star patch into top of cube, taking care to match corners. Stitch with 1 cm seams.
3 Pin second star patch to bottom of letters. Stitch, leaving one side open.
4 Turn fabric cube right way out. Stuff with filling. Fold under 1 cm on opening edges, pin together and stitch.

ALPHABET AND STARS FOR STENCILLING

A B ☆ C

G ☆ H I

M N O ☆

ALPHABET AND STARS FOR STENCILLING

CRIB STARS

Materials

Small pieces of yellow fabric
200 cm white satin ribbon, 1 cm wide
40 cm elastic, 6 mm wide
3 bells
Soft filling

Instructions

1 Cut out six stars from outline on this page. Stitch each pair of stars together on all but one side. Turn and press. Fill. Stitch across openings.

2 Cut ribbon in half. Place wrong sides together; pin one end of elastic 25 cm from ribbon ends. Stitch across elastic and along one side of ribbons to 25 cm from other end. Pull unsecured end of elastic and stitch across, then stitch along other side of ribbons.

3 Attach bells securely to bottom point of star, and attach star to ribbon.

CROSS STITCH SHEET TRIM

Also see page 47 for general instructions on cross stitching.

Materials

DMC Stranded Cotton 744
15-count Aida Band, 4.5 cm wide
 x width of sheet plus 3 cm
Purchased sheet

Instructions

1 Use the charts below.
2 Wash sheet and Aida Band for shrinkage.
3 Mark centre of band with tacking stitch. Using two strands of cotton, stitch stars from centre of chart in both directions until band is complete.
4 Press stitched band from wrong side. Press under 1.5 cm on each end of band; pin to sheet and sew into place.

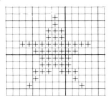

CROSS STITCH TOWEL TRIM

Materials

DMC Stranded Cotton
 (select from colours: 223, 758, 502, 932, 554, 3743, 744)
14-count Aida Band, 8 cm wide x
 width of towel plus 3 cm
Purchased bath towel

Instructions

1 This project uses letters in the sampler chart on pages 54–59 and the star on this page.
2 Wash towel and Aida Band for shrinkage.
3 Using two strands of cotton, stitch centre letter of name at centre of band. If you have an even number of letters, then stitch a star at the centre.
4 Working outwards in each direction, alternate stars and letters until the name is complete.
5 Press stitched band from wrong side. Press under 1.5 cm on each end of band; pin to towel and sew into place.

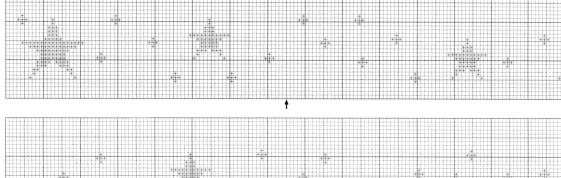

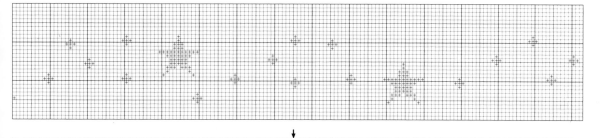

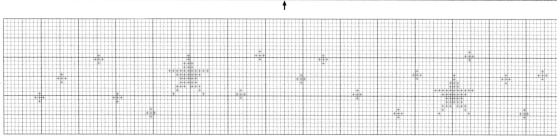

COLOUR KEY

+ yellow 744

Cross stitch sheet trim

CROSS STITCH SAMPLER CHART

CROSS STITCH SAMPLER CHART

COLOUR KEY	
× blue 932	▪ green 502
○ rose 223	▲ lavender 554
\ mauve 9743	+ yellow 744
• apricot 758	

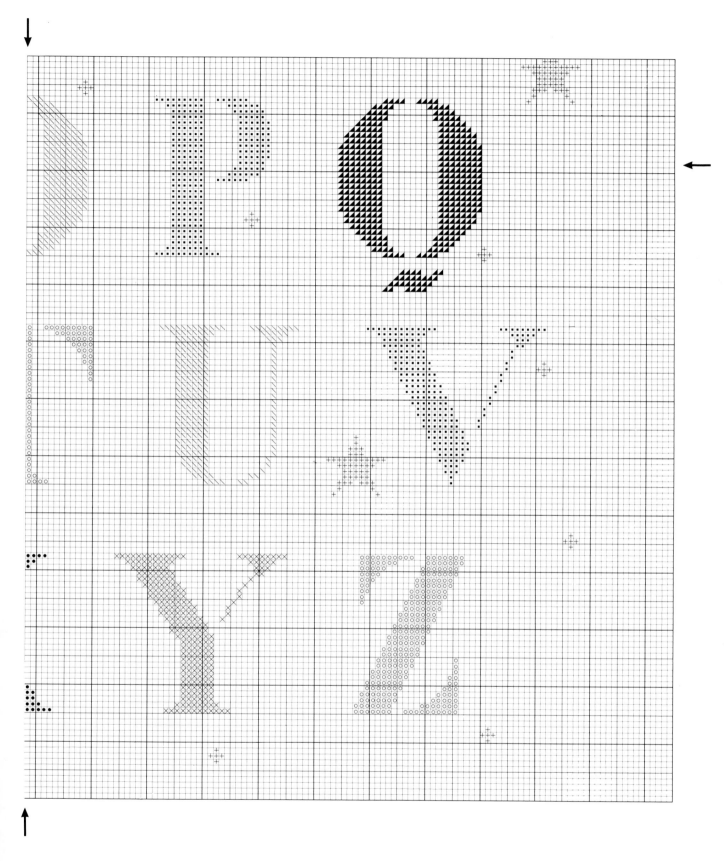

CROSS STITCH SAMPLER CHART

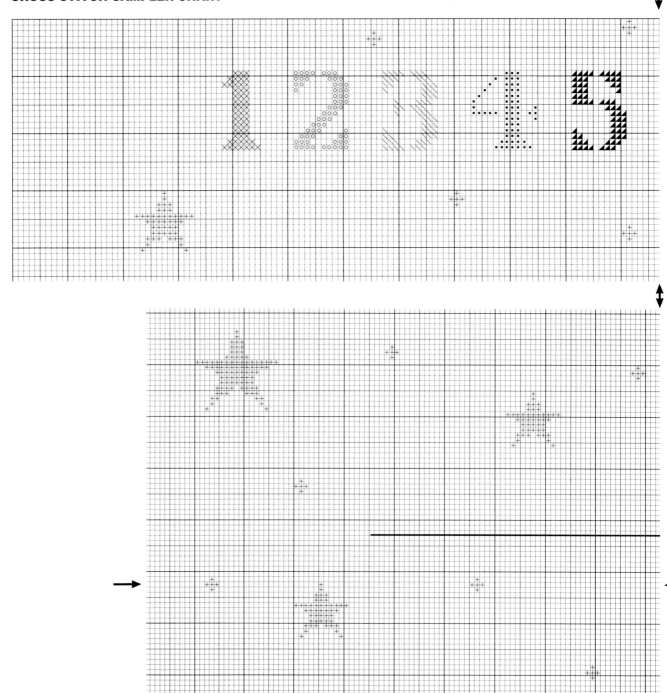

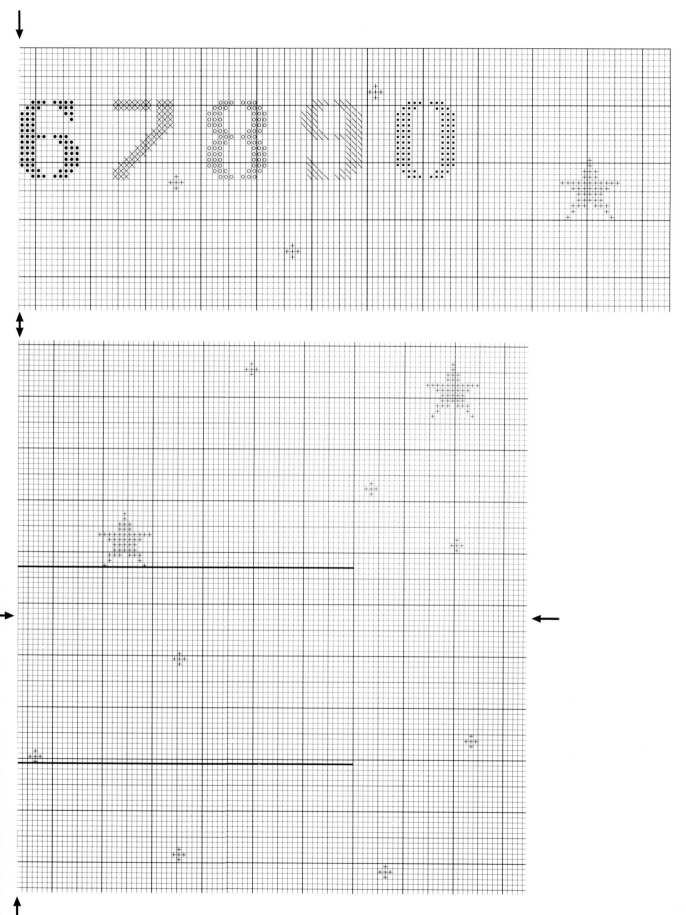

CROSS STITCH SAMPLER

Materials

DMC Stranded Cotton, two
skeins each of:
223, 758, 502, 932, 554, 3743, 744
60 cm x 14-count white perle Aida
(DMC Art 1007), 110 cm wide

Instructions

1 This project uses charts on pages
54–59 and is stitched in two sections: an
upper section with alphabet and stars,
and a personalised lower section with the
child's initials and birthdate. Before
stitching, chart desired initials and date in
the spaces provided, using alphabet and
numbers from upper section and allowing
23 spaces between initials and 15
between numbers. (The panels could also
be framed as two separate projects: the
upper panel as an alphabet sampler and
the lower as a door plaque, for example).

2 Wash Aida for shrinkage; press. Cut
into two sections, one 70 cm long and the
other 40 cm long.

3 Mark centre lines of both pieces of
Aida with tacking threads. There will be
a margin of approximately 10 cm around
finished stitching.

4 Using centre lines on Aida and chart as
your guide, stitch both sections of
sampler with two strands of cotton.

5 Rinse, dry and press both sections.
(If you wash them separately, or wash one
and not the other, you may find slight
variations in the colour).

6 Consult with a picture framer about
the best way to mount the work prior to
framing. Some recommend that stitching
is laced onto a board, others prefer acid-
free taping.

CROSS STITCH BIBS

Materials

DMC Stranded Cotton
(select from colours: 223, 758, 502,
932, 554, 3743, 744)
14-count Borderline Baby Bibs
Small amount of iron-on stiffening

Instructions

1 These projects use letters in sampler
chart on pages 54–59 and the small star on
this page. You could choose to stitch the
child's name, initials or simply ABC.
Check that they will fit in the space
available.

2 Wash bibs for shrinkage.

3 Using two strands of cotton, stitch
letters and stars as desired.

4 Press stitching from wrong side. Cut a
piece of iron-on stiffening just large
enough to cover stitching panel and fuse
to wrong side of bib. This will help the
bib to hang well and also keep the ends
of threads away from little fingers!

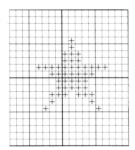

CROSS STITCH RUG

Materials

DMC Stranded Cottons:
223, 758, 502, 932, 554, 3743, 744
Anne Cloth (DMC Art. 7563),
100 x 150 cm (6 x 9 squares)
Soft cotton lining fabric, 100 x 150 cm

Instructions

1 This project uses letters from the
sampler chart on pages 54–59 and the
large star on this page.

2 Wash Anne Cloth and lining for
shrinkage; press.

3 Centring each letter in its square,
stitch in three strands of cotton.

4 Rinse, dry and press.

5 Using zigzag stitch on your machine,
stitch 2 cm in from each side of Anne
Cloth. Remove threads to create frayed
edging.

6 Press 2 cm in on each side of lining
fabric. Pin to back of Anne Cloth and sew
into place.

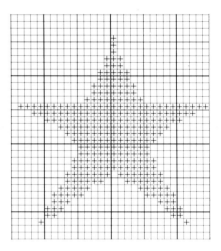

TOPS AND TAILS

Instructions

Make these shorts, buy some plain t-shirts and use the creative ideas on pages 16–19 for lots of different outfits.

SHORTS

Materials

    40 cm cotton knit, 150 cm wide
    50 cm elastic, 2 cm wide

Instructions

1 Cut two of Shorts Front & Back 18. Seam allowances are 1 cm, hem allowances 2 cm.

2 Stitch centre front and centre back seams. Press. Stitch along inside leg seam, matching crutch points. Press.

3 To form casing, turn under 4 cm at waist edge; stitch 3 cm from edge, leaving opening at centre back. Edgestitch close to top edge to neaten. Cut elastic to fit waist, insert and join ends. Stitch across opening.

4 Turn under 1 cm and 1 cm again at hems. Topstitch and edgestitch to finish.

See Machine Appliqué Tips on page 74.

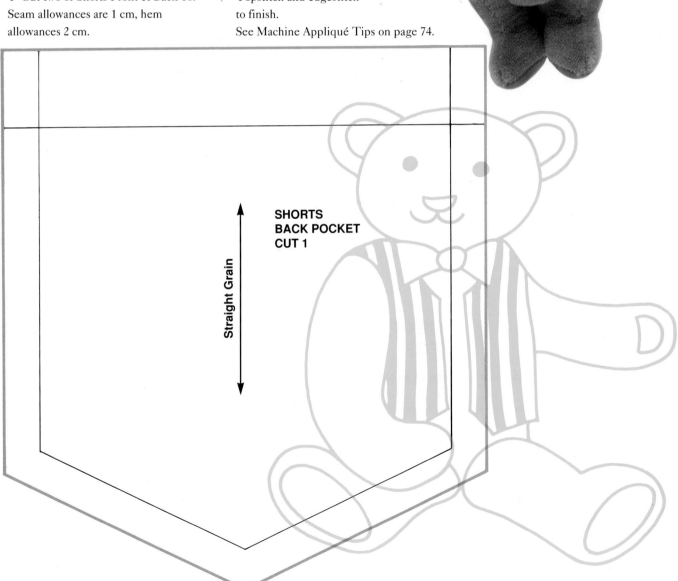

Straight Grain

SHORTS
BACK POCKET
CUT 1

LET'S GO BOATING

Instructions

Unless otherwise stated: seam allowances are 1 cm throughout, hem allowances 3 cm, fabric requirements are for fabrics 115 cm wide, and all pieces should be joined with right sides together. Exposed raw edges on woven fabrics should be neatened by overlock stitching, zigzag stitch or pinking shears and on ribbing by overlock stitching or zigzag. Raw edges of knit fabrics can be left raw as they will not fray. All pattern pieces are on the pull-out pattern sheet at the back of the book. Patterns for this chapter are for sizes 2 and 4. (Size 4 is shown in brackets). For finished sizes of garments and general instructions, see pages 46–47.

RAGLAN TOP

Materials
100 cm striped cotton knit, 150 cm wide
10 cm contrast ribbing, 90 cm wide

Instructions
1 Cut one Front 1, one Back 2 and two Sleeve 3 pieces in size 2 or 4 as required.
2 From ribbing, cut neckband 6 cm x 30 cm (32 cm) and two pieces for sleeve piping each 3 cm x 40 cm (45 cm).
3 Stitch underarm seams on sleeves. Press. Stitch front to back at side seams. Press.

4 Fold piping strips in half lengthways, with wrong sides together. Pin strips to right side of armhole, raw edges together, stretching slightly. Baste. Pin sleeves to armhole over piping. Stitch through all thicknesses. Press seams away from sleeves.
5 Stitch ends of neck ribbing together to form loop. Fold in half, seam inside. Pin evenly around neck edge, raw edges together and ribbing seam at centre back. Stitch with zigzag or overlocking to allow neck opening to stretch sufficiently. Press seam away from ribbing.
6 Turn under 1.5 cm then 1.5 cm again at hem. Topstitch and edgestitch. Repeat for sleeve hems.

CROPPED RAGLAN TOP

Materials
50 cm striped cotton knit, 150 cm wide
10 cm contrast ribbing, 90 cm wide

Instructions
1 Cut one Front 1, one Back 2 and two Sleeve 3 pieces in size 2 or 4 as required.
2 From ribbing, cut neckband 6 cm x 30 cm (32 cm) and two pieces for sleeve piping each 3 cm x 40 cm (45 cm).
3 Stitch underarm seams on sleeves.

Press. Stitch front to back at side seams. Press.
4 Fold piping strips in half lengthways, with wrong sides together. Pin strips to right side of armhole, raw edges together, stretching slightly. Baste. Pin sleeves to armhole over piping. Stitch through all thicknesses. Press seams away from sleeves.
5 Stitch ends of neck ribbing together to form loop. Fold in half, seam inside. Pin evenly around neck edge, raw edges together and ribbing seam at centre back. Stitch with zigzag or overlocking to allow neck opening to stretch sufficiently. Press seam away from ribbing.
6 Turn under 1.5 cm then 1.5 cm again at hem. Topstitch and edgestitch. Repeat for sleeve hems.

PANEL SHORTS

Materials
60 cm wide stripe cotton
50 cm elastic, 2 cm wide

Instructions
1 Cut two pieces each of Centre Front 7, Lower Side/Pocket 8, Upper Side/Pocket 9 and Back 10 in size 2 or 4 as required. Hem allowance is 2 cm.
2 Fold lower side/pocket along line indicated for top of pocket; press. Pin to upper side/pocket, matching pocket bottoms. Baste.
3 Stitch centre fronts to completed side/pocket sections. Press seams to centre.
4 Stitch backs to completed side/pocket sections. Press seams to back.
5 Stitch centre front and centre back seams. Press. Stitch along inside leg seam, matching crutch points. Press.
6 To form casing, turn over 1 cm then 3 cm at top; stitch, leaving opening. Edgestitch close to top of shorts.
7 Turn under 1 cm and 1 cm again at hems. Topstitch and edgestitch.
8 Cut elastic to fit waist, insert and join ends. Stitch across opening.

PANEL PANTS

Materials

100 cm cotton drill
50 cm elastic, 2 cm wide

Instructions

1 Cut two pieces each of Centre Front 7, Lower Side/Pocket 8, Upper Side/Pocket 9 and Back 10 in size 2 or 4 as required. Hem allowance is 2 cm.

2 Fold lower side/pocket along line indicated for top of pocket; press. Pin to upper side/pocket, matching pocket bottoms. Baste.

3 Stitch centre fronts to completed side/pocket sections. Press seams to centre.

4 Stitch backs to completed side/pocket sections. Press seams to back.

5 Stitch centre front and centre back seams. Press. Stitch along inside leg seam, matching crutch points. Press.

6 To form casing, turn over 1 cm then 3 cm at top; stitch, leaving opening. Edgestitch close to top of shorts.

7 Turn under 1 cm and 1 cm again at hems. Topstitch and edgestitch.

8 Cut elastic to fit waist, insert and join ends. Stitch across opening.

SKIRT

Materials

30 cm (40 cm) spot cotton knit,
  150 cm wide
20 cm contrast stripe cotton knit,
  150 cm wide
50 cm elastic, 2 cm wide

Instructions

1 Cut skirt from spot fabric, 30 cm (32 cm) x 150 cm. Cut hem from stripe fabric, 16 cm (18 cm) x 150 cm.

2 Stitch side seams of skirt and hem sections; press. Fold hem section in half lengthways, with wrong sides together. Press and baste. Mark upper edge of hem section and lower edge of skirt in quarters; pin together evenly, matching markings and side seams. Stitch; press to skirt.

3 To form casing, turn under 4 cm at top of skirt; press. Stitch 3 cm from top of

skirt, leaving opening at centre back. Edgestitch close to top of skirt. Cut elastic to fit waist, insert and join ends. Stitch across opening.

SAILOR TOP

Materials

80 cm navy blue cotton knit,
  150 cm wide
10 cm matching ribbing, 90 cm wide
Small piece of striped cotton knit
  for V-neck
100 cm decorative braid or
  ribbon, 3 cm wide

Instructions

1 Cut one Front 1, one Back 2, two Sleeves 3, two Collars 4 and one Tie 5 from navy cotton knit. Cut one V neck 6 from striped knit. Cut ribbing 6 cm x 30 cm (32 cm).

2 Stitch sleeves to front and back along armhole seams.

3 Stitch collar pieces together around outside edge. Trim seams and corners;

turn and press. Pin braid around edge of collar, mitring corners; stitch. Press.

4 Pin collar to neck edge, matching notches. Stitch. Snip seam allowance at centre front to stitching at V.

5 Matching raw edges, pin striped V section to neck and collar; stitch.

6 Stitch ends of neck ribbing together to form loop. Fold in half, seam inside. Pin evenly around neck edge through collar and V section, with raw edges together and ribbing seam at centre back. Stitch with zigzag or overlocking to allow neck opening to stretch sufficiently. Press seam away from ribbing.

7 Stitch front to back at underarm seams, matching underarm points. Press.

8 Stitch braid or ribbon across ends of tie. Fold tie in half lengthways; stitch, leaving a small opening. Trim seams, turn and press. Knot gently and handstitch under collar.

9 Turn under 1.5 cm then 1.5 cm again at hem. Topstitch and edgestitch. Repeat for sleeve hems.

STRETCH KNIT TIPS

Before cutting, always wash and dry fabrics as they will be treated when made into garments; if you intend to tumble dry the garment, then tumble dry the fabric first. Part of the appeal of stretch fabric is that it requires virtually no ironing if handled with a little care. Cut pattern pieces paying attention to grain lines.

Another feature of stretch knits is that they do not fray, so edges need no special finishing. However, ribbing can unravel, so remember to neaten edges by overlock stitching or zigzag.

And here's a tip to keep seams staying neat, and to save on ironing too. After stitching, press seam to one side and edgestitch 2 mm from seam. Line up the seam with a marking on your presser foot for easy, even stitching. This finish works equally well on stretch knits and woven fabrics.

For stretch or knit fabric, use your machine's narrowest zigzag stitch for all sewing so that seams and edges will have sufficient 'give' and the stitching won't break when stretched. Your machine may have a special stitch for stretch fabrics, so practise with this before trying it on a garment. Sewers who still prefer a straight stitch should stretch the seam slightly as they sew to achieve the same 'give'.

Make sure your needle is new, because old and blunt needles can ladder knits, and always use a good quality polyester thread.

SAILOR DRESS

Materials

        60 cm spotted cotton knit, 150 cm wide
        60 cm striped cotton knit, 150 cm wide
        10 cm ribbing, 90 cm wide

Instructions

1 From spotted knit cut one Front 1, one Back 2, two Sleeves 3 and one V Neck 6. From striped knit cut two collars 4, one Tie 5 and a piece for skirt 20 cm (22 cm) x 150 cm. Cut ribbing 6 cm x 30 cm (32 cm).

2 Stitch sleeves to front and back along armhole seams.

3 Stitch collar pieces together around outside edge. Trim seams and corners; turn and press.

4 Pin collar to neck edge, matching notches. Stitch. Snip seam allowance at centre front to stitching at V.

5 Matching raw edges, pin V section to neck and collar; stitch.

6 Stitch ends of neck ribbing together to form loop. Fold in half, seam inside. Pin evenly around neck edge through collar and V section, with raw edges together and ribbing seam at centre back. Stitch with zigzag or overlocking to allow neck opening to stretch sufficiently. Press seam away from ribbing.

7 Stitch front to back at underarm seams, matching underarm points. Press.

8 Fold tie in half lengthways; stitch, leaving a small opening. Trim seams, turn and press. Knot gently and handstitch under collar.

9 Stitch side seam of skirt. Press. Mark top and skirt waist edges into quarters. Gather top of skirt, then pin evenly around waist edge, matching markings and with skirt seam at left side. Stitch and press.

10 Turn under 1.5 cm then 1.5 cm again at hem. Topstitch and edgestitch. Repeat for sleeve hems.

NAVY AND RED HAT

Materials

        40 cm x 50 cm navy cotton drill
        20 cm x 30 cm red cotton drill
        50 cm tartan
        red thread

Instructions

1 Cut three Crown 11 pieces in navy and three in red. Cut one Brim 12 piece in navy and another in tartan. Cut bias band from tartan, 3 cm x 60 cm.

2 Stitch crown pieces together along curved sides, matching points at centre. Press. Repeat for crown lining.

3 Stitch centre back seam of brims. Press. Stitch navy brim to tartan brim around outside edge. Trim and clip seams, turn and press. Starting from outside edge, topstitch in red in a continuous spiral to inside edge, with stitching rows approximately 8 mm apart.

4 Mark brim and crown edges into quarters. With wrong sides facing, pin together matching markings. Stitch. Trim seams.

5 Bind seam on outside with bias band to neaten raw edges. Topstitch to crown.

STRIPED HAT

Materials

        50 cm wide striped cotton fabric
        40 cm x 70 cm white cotton

Instructions

1 Cut six Crown 11 pieces in each fabric. Cut one Brim 12 piece in each fabric.

2 Stitch crown pieces together along curved sides, matching points at centre. Press. Repeat for crown lining.

3 Stitch centre back seam of brims. Press. Stitch navy brim to tartan brim around outside edge. Trim and clip seams, turn and press. Starting from outside edge, topstitch in red in a continuous spiral to inside edge, with stitching rows approximately 8 mm apart.

4 Mark brim and crown edges into quarters. With wrong sides facing, pin together matching markings. Stitch. Trim seams.

5 Bind seam on outside with bias band to neaten raw edges. Topstitch to crown.

ANCHOR KNIT CHART

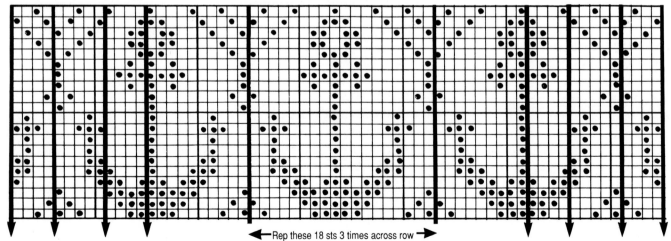

Size 4   Size 3   Size 2   Size 1   ←Rep these 18 sts 3 times across row →   Size 1   Size 2   Size 3   Size 4

● MC   ☐ C1

ANCHOR KNIT TOP

See measurements for different sizes on page 47.

Materials

Thorobred's 4 Ply Crochet and Knitting Cotton (50g) balls:

Size		1	2	3	4
(Navy)	MC	1	1	1	2
(White)	C1	1	1	1	2
(Red)	C2	1	1	1	1

1 pair 2.75 mm (No.12) knitting needles

1 pair 3 mm (No.11) knitting needles

1 pair 3.25 mm (No.10) knitting needles

2 stitch holders

Size 1and 2 only - 3 buttons

Instructions

TENSION:

28 sts to 10cm over st st, using 3.25 mm needles.

BACK:

Using 2.75 mm needles and MC, cast on 73 (81, 91, 99) sts.

1st Row: (wrong side) Knit.

Rep 1st row until band measures 2 (2.5, 3, 3) cm from beg, working last row on wrong side.

Change to 3.25 mm needles.

Using C1, work 0 (8, 8, 12) rows in st st (1 row K, 1 row P).

Using C2, work 0 (2, 2, 2) rows in st st.

Cont in st st and stripes of 8 (8, 8, 12) rows MC, 2 rows C2 and 2 rows C1.

** Change to 3 mm needles.

Work rows 1 to 20 inclusive from graph using Fair Isle method.

Change to 3.25 mm needles. **

Cont in st st and stripes of 2 rows C1, 2 rows C2, 8 (8, 8, 12) rows MC, 2 rows C2 and 2 rows C1.

Rep from ** to **.

Cont in st st and stripes of 2 rows C1, 2 rows C2, 6 (8, 8, 12) rows MC, 0 (0, 2, 2) rows C2, and 0 (0, 6, 6) rows C1.

SHAPE SHOULDERS:

Using MC (MC, C1, C1), cast off 11 (13, 15, 17) sts at beg of next 2 rows, then 12 (13, 15, 17) sts at beg of foll 2 rows.

Leave rem 27 (29, 31, 31) sts on a stitch holder.

FRONT:

Work as given for Back until there are 22(22, 24, 26) rows fewer than Back before 'shape shoulders'.

SHAPE NECK:

Next Row: (right side) Patt 28 (31, 35, 39), turn.

*** Keeping patt correct, dec one st at neck edge in foll alt rows 5 times.

23 (26, 30, 34) sts.

Work 3 (3, 13, 15) rows in patt and stripes. ***

NOTE: This side of neck is 8 rows shorter than other side to accommodate shoulder bands for SIZE 1 and 2 only.

SHAPE SHOULDER:

Cast off 11 (13, 15, 17) sts at beg of next row. Work 1 row.

Cast off.

Slip next 17 (19, 21, 21) sts at centre front onto a stitch holder and leave.

With right side facing, join yarn to rem sts and patt to end.

Work from *** to ***.

Work 9 (9, 1, 1) row/s in patt and stripes.

SHAPE SHOULDER:

Work as for other side.

SLEEVES:

Using 2.75 mm needles and MC, cast on 61 (67, 75, 81) sts.

1st Row: (wrong side) Knit.

Rep 1st row until band measures 2 (2.5, 2.5, 2.5) cm from beg, working last row on wrong side.

Change to 3.25mm needles.

Cont in st st and stripes of 8 rows C1, 2 rows C2 and 0 (0, 2, 4) rows MC.

SHAPE TOP:

Using MC, cast off 6 (7, 7, 8) sts at beg of next 6 rows.

Cast off rem sts.

NECKBAND:

Using back stitch, join right shoulder seam. With right side facing, using 2.75 mm needles and MC, beg at front left shoulder, knit up 72 (75, 89, 92) sts evenly around neck edge (including sts from stitch holders).

1st Row: Knit.

Rep 1st row 8 times more.

Cast off.

Sizes 1 and 2 only:

FRONT SHOULDER BAND:

With right side facing, using 2.75 mm needles and MC, knit up 26 (29) sts evenly along front left shoulder and Neckband.

1st Row: Knit.

Rep 1st row twice more.

Next Row: K3 (6), (cast off 2 sts, K7) twice, cast off 2 sts, K3.

Next Row: K3, cast on 2 sts, (K7, cast on 2 sts) twice,K3 (6).

Knit 4 rows. Cast off.

BACK SHOULDER BAND:

Work as for Front Shoulder band, omitting buttonholes. Place Front Shoulder Band over Back Shoulder Band and catch together at armhole edge.

Sizes 3 and 4 only:

Using back stitch, join left shoulder and Neckband seam.

To make up for all sizes:

Using back stitch, sew in sleeves (armhole depth 10.5 (11.5, 13, 14) cm), then join side and sleeve seams. Sew on buttons for size 1 and 2.

HOME SWEET HOME

Instructions

Unless otherwise stated: seam allowances are 1 cm throughout, hem allowances 3 cm, fabric requirements are for fabrics 115 cm wide, and all pieces should be joined with right sides together. Exposed raw edges on woven fabrics and ribbing should be neatened by overlock stitching, zigzag stitch or pinking shears. For general instructions on sewing, refer to page 46. Also see Machine Appliqué Tips on page 74.

BUTTONED HOUSE CUSHION

Finished size 53 cm square

Materials

> 20 cm main tartan
> 60 cm coordinating fabric
> 35 cm square white background fabric
> Small pieces of fabric for house three buttons
> cushion, 55 cm square

Instructions

1 Cut main tartan into two medium strips, 7 cm x 45 cm, and two long strips, 7 cm x 55 cm. Cut coordinating fabric into two short strips, 7 cm x 35 cm, two medium strips, 7 cm x 45 cm, and two back sections, 38 cm x 55 cm.

2 Using the large outline on page 70, make up a house patch as follows:

a) Cut one each of roof (C), house (D) and small heart (E) from contrasting fabrics. Note that house (D) is cut as a solid rectangle and the small heart (E) is then appliquéd onto it.

b) Cut one whole house plus one small heart (E) from fusible webbing.

c) Trace one whole house onto appliqué backing paper; cut 2 cm larger all round.

d) Fuse and appliqué the small heart (E) onto the centre of each house (D), following directions above.

e) Place a webbing house paper side down on ironing board. Arrange house (D) and roof (C) on top, overlapping by 2 mm at joins. Fuse.

STENCILLED PLAYMAT

(See also Stencilling Tips on page 49)

Materials

> White canvas, 130 cm square
> FolkArt Acrylic Colors:
>> Ultramarine 720
>> Plantation Green 604
>> Calico Red 932
> FolkArt Acrylic Sealer
> FolkArt Water Base Varnish
> Piece of tartan, 24 cm x 130 cm
> Craft glue

Instructions

1 Turn under 4 cm on all edges of canvas. Stitch with zigzag.

2 Cut tartan into four strips 2 cm x 130 cm and eight strips 2 cm x 85 cm.

3 Mark grid on canvas by ruling lines 18.5 cm in from each edge, then dividing centre section into 25 squares of 17 cm each.

4 Prepare stencils according to instructions on page 48, using small heart and house outlines on page 67.

5 Stencil mat. Allow to dry completely.

6 Apply tartan strips using craft glue. Cover playmat with at least two coats of varnish.

STENCILLED CHALKBOARD

Materials

> Stencils cut for playmat
> FolkArt Acrylic Colors:
>> Ultramarine 720
>> Plantation Green 604
>> Calico Red 932
> FolkArt Acrylic Sealer
> FolkArt Antiquing
> Timber-framed chalkboard

Instructions

1 Seal and 'antique' timber frame according to manufacturer's instructions.

2 Stencil across top of chalkboard. Allow to dry completely before handling.

f) Peel paper away from fusing, centre house on white patch, fuse.

g) Pin backing paper to back of patch. Starting at star and following the direction indicated on the outline (page 70), use a close zigzag (satin stitch) to machine appliqué through all thicknesses. Tear away backing paper. .

3 Join short coordinating strips to top and bottom of patch, then medium coordinating strips to each side. Then join medium tartan strips to top and bottom, and finally long tartan strips to either side to complete cushion front.

4 On one long side of each back section, turn under 1 cm then 6 cm. Stitch. Make three buttonholes along one of these finished sides.

5 With right sides facing, pin section with buttonholes to one side of cushion front, then overlap other section and pin in position. Stitch. Neaten all seams, turn and press. Sew on buttons. Insert cushion.

HEART CUSHION WITH BOWS

Finished size 53 cm square

Materials

    100 cm main tartan
    20 cm coordinating fabric
    35 cm square white background fabric
    Small pieces of fabric for heart
        cushion, 55 cm square

Instructions

1 Cut main tartan into pieces as follows:
two medium strips, 7 cm x 45 cm;
two long strips, 7 cm x 55 cm;
one facing strip, 14 cm x 108 cm;six ties, 7 cm x 35 cm and a back, 55 cm square.
Cut coordinating fabric as follows:
two short strips, 7 cm x 35 cm;
two medium strips, 7 cm x 45 cm

2 Using the large outline (page 70), make up a heart patch as follows:

a) Cut two tops (A) and one bottom (B) from contrasting fabrics.

b) Cut one whole heart from fusible webbing.

c) Trace one whole heart onto appliqué backing paper; cut 2 cm larger all round.

d) Place a webbing heart paper side down on ironing board. Arrange two tops (A) and a bottom (B) on top to form heart, overlapping by 2 mm at joins. Fuse according to manufacturer's instructions.

e) Peel paper away from fusing, centre heart on white patch, fuse.

f) Pin backing paper to back of patch. Starting at star and following the direction indicated on the outline (page 70), use a close zigzag (satin stitch) to machine appliqué through all thicknesses. Tear away backing paper. For more information, see Machine Appliqué Tips on page 74.

3 Join short coordinating strips to top and bottom of patch, then medium coordinating strips to each side. Then join medium tartan strips to top and bottom, and finally long tartan strips to either side to complete cushion front.

4 With right sides together, stitch front to back along three sides, leaving right side open. Turn and press.

5 Turn under 5 mm then 5 mm again on long sides and one end of each tie. Stitch.

6 Sew ends of facing together to form loop. Turn under 5 mm then 5 mm again of one long edge. Stitch.

7 With right sides facing and raw edges together, pin three ties along right side of cushion front. Pin three remaining ties in corresponding positions on back. Then pin unfinished edge of facing over cushion edge and ties. Stitch through all thicknesses. Neaten all seams. Turn and press facing to inside. Edgestitch to keep facing and ties in place. Insert cushion.

PILLOWSLIP

Finished size 38 cm x 58 cm

Materials

    135 cm x 40 cm white background
        fabric
    7 cm x 40 cm strip of main tartan
    Small pieces of coordinating fabric
    Matching thread

Instructions

1 On both ends of white fabric, turn under 1 cm then 1 cm again; stitch.

2 Turn under 1 cm along long sides of tartan strip. Pin strip 17 cm in from one finished end of white fabric; edgestitch.

3 Using the middle-sized outline on page 68, make up a house patch as follows:

a) Cut one each of roof (C), house (D) and small heart (E) from contrasting fabrics. Note that house (D) is cut as a solid rectangle and the small heart (E) is then appliquéd onto it.

b) Cut one whole house plus one small heart (E) from fusible webbing.

c) Trace one whole house onto appliqué backing paper; cut 2 cm larger all round.

d) Fuse and appliqué the small heart (E) onto the centre of each house (D), following directions above.

e) Place a webbing house paper side down on ironing board. Arrange house (D) and roof (C) on top, overlapping by 2 mm at joins. Fuse.

f) Peel paper away from fusing, centre house on white patch, fuse.

g) Pin backing paper to back of patch. Starting at star and following the direction indicated on the outline (page 70), use a close zigzag (satin stitch) to machine appliqué through all thicknesses. Tear away backing paper. For more information, see Machine Appliqué Tips on page 74.

Position the house patch 28 cm to the left of tartan strip and 4 cm from top of fabric; fuse and appliqué according to earlier instructions.

4 Fold back 58 cm from end without tartan strip, right sides facing so that tartan strip and house are now inside envelope. Then fold back 15 cm flap. Pin; stitch both seams. Neaten all seams. Turn and press.

CURTAIN SASHES

Materials

Two strips of main tartan, each
40 cm x 230 cm
Matching thread

Instructions

1 Fold end of strip in half. Press end to fold to form an angle of 45 degrees. Cut along pressed line. Repeat with other three ends.
2 Fold whole strip in half lengthways. Stitch edges together, leaving an opening of 30 cm.
3 Turn and press. Stitch across opening.

FITTED COT SHEET

To fit mattress 70 cm x 130 cm x 10 cm

Materials

180 cm fabric
140 cm elastic, 6 mm wide

Instructions

1 Cut fabric to 174 cm x 114 cm. Cut 10 cm squares out of each corner.
2 With right sides facing, pin cut edges together; stitch. Neaten edges.
3 Turn under 5 mm then 1 cm on all edges. Stitch close to first fold to form elastic casing, leaving openings along sides 20 cm from each corner.
4 Cut elastic in half. Thread one piece through top casing and one through bottom; secure at openings.

DOONA COVER

Finished size 95 cm x 110 cm. Seam allowance 1 cm. Refer to construction diagram for more information.

Materials

70 cm main tartan
20 cm each of six coordinating fabrics
160 cm white background fabric
70 cm paper-backed fusible webbing
70 cm appliqué backing paper
20 cm velcro strip
20 cm x 30 cm sheet of sandpaper

Instructions

1 Transfer the middle-size house and heart outlines on this page onto sandpaper and cut out individual pieces to use as templates. Mark templates with letters A to E as indicated. (Thick card or plastic can be used in place of sandpaper).
2 Preshrink all fabrics by washing. Cut nine 27 cm squares from background fabric.
3 Make five heart patches as follows:
a) Cut ten tops (A) and five bottoms (B) from contrasting fabrics.
b) Cut five whole hearts from fusible webbing.
c) Trace five whole hearts onto appliqué backing paper; cut 2 cm larger all round.
d) Place a webbing heart paper side down on ironing board. Arrange two tops (A) and a bottom (B) on top to form heart, overlapping by 2 mm at joins. Fuse according to manufacturer's instructions.
e) Peel paper away from fusing, centre heart on white patch, fuse.
f) Pin backing paper to back of patch. Starting at star and following the direction indicated on the outline (this page), use a close zigzag (satin stitch) to machine appliqué through all thicknesses. Tear away backing paper. For more information, see Machine Appliqué Tips on page 74.
4 Make four house patches as follows:
a) Cut four each of roof (C), house (D) and small heart (E) from contrasting fabrics. Note that house (D) is cut as a solid rectangle and the small heart (E) is then appliquéd onto it.
b) Cut four whole houses plus four small hearts (E) from fusible webbing.
c) Trace four whole houses onto appliqué backing paper; cut 2 cm larger all round.
d) Fuse and appliqué the small hearts (E) onto the centre of each house (D), following directions above.
e) Place a webbing house paper side down on ironing board. Arrange house (D) and roof (C) on top, overlapping by 2 mm at joins. Fuse.

f) Peel paper away from fusing, centre house on white patch, fuse.
g) Pin backing paper to back of patch. Starting at star and following the direction indicated on the outline (this page), use a close zigzag (satin stitch) to machine appliqué through all thicknesses. Tear away backing paper. For more information, see Machine Appliqué Tips on page 74.
5 Make up as follows:
a) Cut main tartan into 12 strips:
6 short channels (F) 7 cm x 27 cm
2 long channels (G) 7 cm x 87 cm
1 top (H) 22 cm x 87 cm
1 bottom (I) 7 cm x 87 cm
1 left side (J) 7 cm x 112 cm
1 right side (K) 11 cm x 112 cm
b) Referring to construction diagram (opposite), take patches 1, 2 and 3 and join with two short channels (F). Repeat for patches 4, 5 and 6 and patches 7, 8 and 9 to make three long strips.
c) Join these three strips with the two long channels (G).
Then add top (H), bottom (I) and sides (J and K) to complete upper section of doona cover.
d) Cut piece for lower section of doona cover from background fabric, 97 cm x 116 cm. On right side of upper section and one side of lower section, turn under 1 cm then another 2 cm; edgestitch.
e) With right sides facing, join upper and lower sections, using a 2 cm seam on finished side and 1 cm seam on the other three sides, leaving an opening of 60 cm on finished side.
Neaten all seams; turn and press. Cut velcro into four strips each 5 cm long. Attach to 2 cm finished seam allowances inside doona cover.

DOONA COVER CONSTRUCTION DIAGRAM

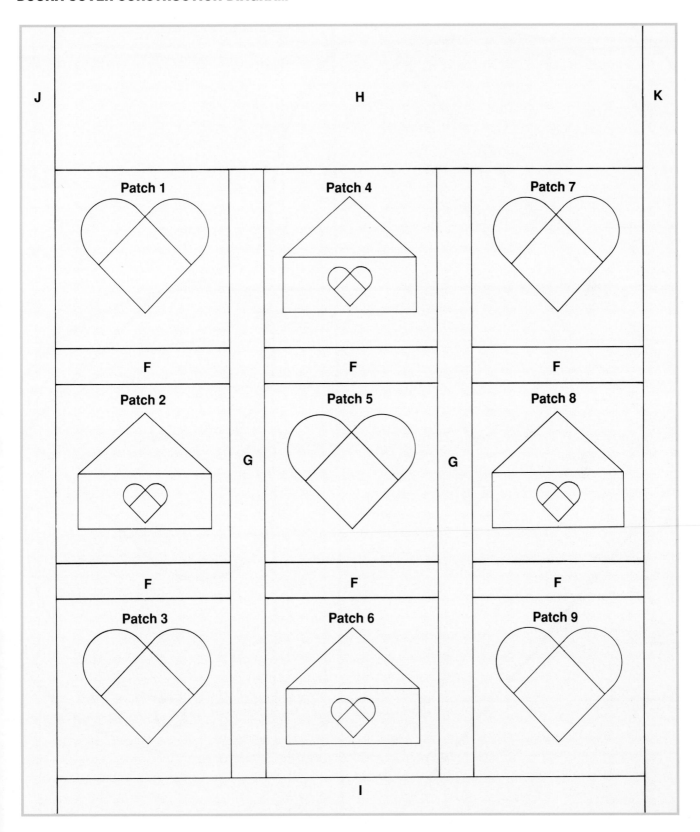

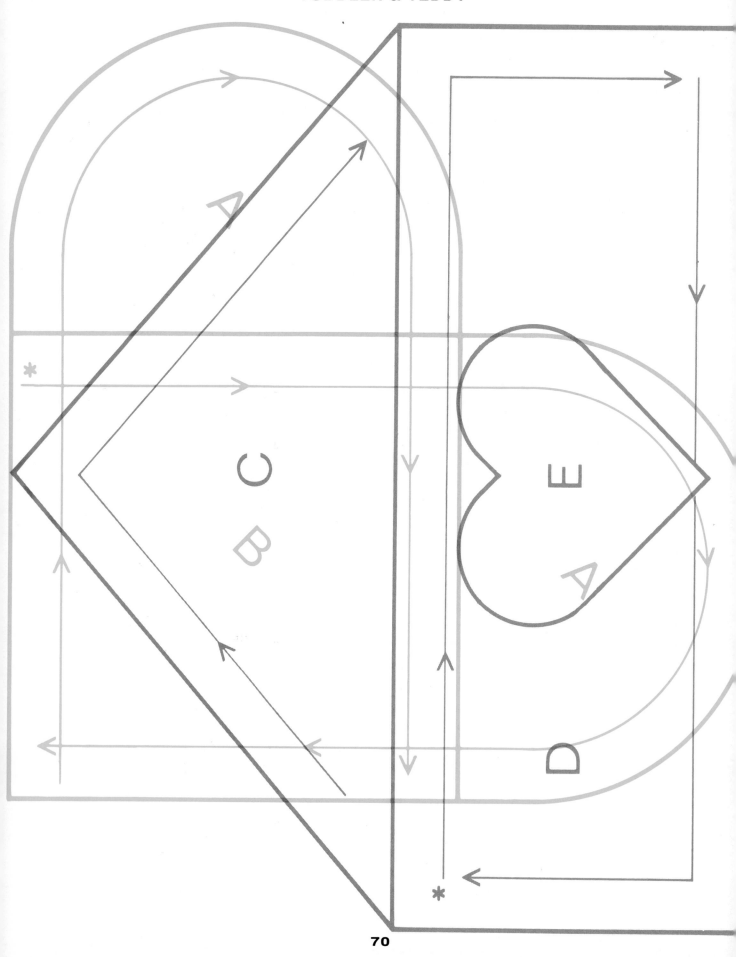

PYJAMAS

Materials

- 100 cm tartan fabric
- 10 cm contrast cotton ribbing, 90 cm wide
- 50 cm elastic, 2 cm wide

Instructions

1 Using pattern pieces from pattern sheet, cut one Front 13, one Back 14, two Sleeves 15 and two Shorts Front & Back 18. Cut V-neck in Front 13, as indicated.

2 Stitch shoulder seams. Press. Fold ribbing in half lengthways and pin one end to right side of V, with raw edges together and ribbing extending 3 cm beyond point of V. Continue pinning around neck edge, stretching ribbing more at back, and overlapping ribbing at V. Stitch through all layers, starting 4 cm up right side from V and finishing at left side 6 mm below V.

3 Snip seam allowance at V to stitching. Press seam away from ribbing and tuck right end of ribbing inside pyjama top, then cross left end over. Pin at overlap. Stitch remaining 4 cm on right side. Stitch right end of ribbing to seam allowance on left of V. Trim ribbing beyond overlap.

4 Stitch sleeves to armholes. Press. Stitch front to back along underarm seams, matching underarm points. Press.

5 Turn under 1.5 cm and 1.5 cm again at hem. Topstitch and edgestitch to finish. Repeat for sleeve hems.

6 Stitch centre front and centre back seams of pyjama bottoms. Press. Stitch along inside leg seam, matching crutch points. Press.

7 To form casing, turn under 1 cm then 3 cm at waist edge; stitch, leaving opening at centre back. Edgestitch close to top edge to neaten. Cut elastic to fit waist, insert and join ends. Stitch across opening.

8 Turn under 1 cm and 1 cm again at hems. Topstitch and edgestitch to finish.

NEEDLEPOINT KEEPSAKE HOUSE

Materials

- 2 x plastic canvas mats, 30 cm x 45 cm (DMC Art. No. SW709)
- DMC Laine Colbert tapestry wool in these colours and skein quantities:
  - Red 7544 (5)
  - Green 7943 (2)
  - Blue 7317 (3)
  - Turquoise 7595 (3)
  - Mid Grey 7288 (5)
  - Dark Grey 7289 (2)
- **Tapestry needle**
- **6 cm x 12 cm felt**
- **Craft glue**

Instructions

1 Refer to the chart on page 72: From one plastic canvas mat, cut house front and back each 74 x 26 squares (approximately 28 cm x 10 cm) and roof front and back each 74 x 34 squares (28 cm x 13 cm). From second mat cut two house sides each 36 x 26 squares (14 cm x 10 cm), two roof ends each 36 x 46 squares (14 cm x 18 cm) and bottom of house 74 x 36 squares (28 cm x 14 cm). Mark all pieces. The roof pieces should be kept as squares for stitching, then trimmed to shape later.

2 Referring to chart on page 72 and general information on page 47, stitch all pieces.

3 Join all four house sides and bottom using 7288, two stitches into each hole. Overcast top edge of house in 7288, one stitch per hole.

4 Trim roof sections to shape, being careful not to cut through any square containing a stitch. Join roof pieces and overcast bottom edge using 7544.

5 Make a twisted cord by dividing remaining 7544 into three, twisting tightly then doubling over. Apply over roof seams with craft glue.

6 Cut felt into two squares. Apply glue and stick to back of house and roof to form hinges.

TODDLER & TEDDY

NEEDLEPOINT HOUSE CHART

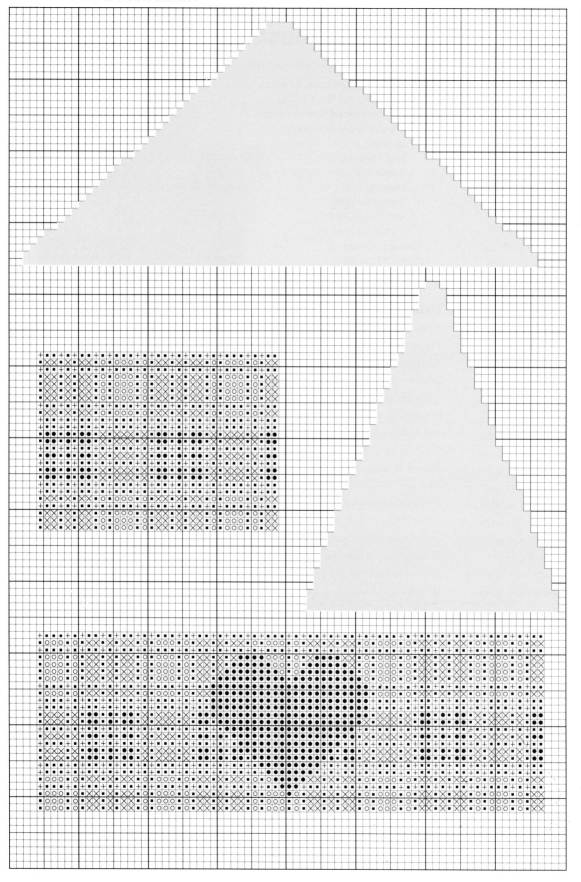

COLOUR KEY

+ dark grey 7289
× Turquoise 7595
• mid grey 7288
● green 7943
○ blue 7317
■ red 7544

FUN IN THE SUN
Instructions

Unless otherwise stated: seam allowances are 1 cm throughout, hem allowances 3 cm, fabric requirements are for fabrics 115 cm wide, and all pieces should be joined with right sides together. Exposed raw edges on ribbing should be neatened by overlock stitching or zigzag stitch. Raw edges of knit fabrics can be left raw as they will not fray. All pattern pieces are found on the pull-out pattern sheet at the back of the book. Patterns for this chapter are for sizes 1 and 3. (Size 3 is shown in brackets). For finished sizes of garments and general instructions, refer to page 46. See Stretch Knit Tips on page 63 and Machine Appliqué Tips on page 74.

WIDE-BRIMMED HAT

Materials
40 cm x 50 cm main cotton knit
20 cm x 30 cm contrast cotton knit
40 cm x 70 cm cotton knit print
Bias band

Instructions
1 Cut three Crowns 11 in main colour, three in contrast and six in print. Cut Brim 12 in main colour and print. Cut strip 3 cm x 60 cm across width of print fabric. Seam and edge allowances are 1 cm.
2 Stitch crown pieces together along

curved sides, matching points at centre. Press. Repeat for crown lining.
3 Stitch centre back seam of brim. Press. Repeat for brim lining. Stitch brim to lining around outside edge. Trim and clip seams, turn and press. Starting from outside edge, topstitch in a continuous spiral to inside edge, with stitching rows approximately 8 mm apart.
4 Mark brim and crown edges into quarters. With wrong sides facing, pin together matching markings. Stitch. Trim seams.
5 Bind seam on outside with bias band to neaten raw edges. Topstitch to crown.

BOY'S SWIMSUIT

Materials
20 cm cotton/lycra two-way
stretch fabric, 60 cm wide
100 cm swimsuit elastic, 1 cm wide
Small pieces of contrast cotton
knits for appliqué

Instructions
1 Cut one each of Front 19 and Back 20. 6 mm seams and 1 cm edges allowed.
2 Stitch left side seam. Press.
3 Prepare appliqué patches using the small fish on this page. Refer to Machine Appliqué Tips on page 74. Position as

desired from front to back across left side seam. Appliqué. Finish with machine embroidery as desired.
4 Stitch right side seam and crutch seam. Press.
5 Cut elastic to fit snugly around waist. Join ends. Mark waist edge and elastic into quarters. Pin elastic evenly around wrong side of waist edge, matching markings. Stitch in place using zigzag to allow elasticised edge to stretch. Turn under 1 cm at waist edge, zigzag stitch to finish. Repeat for leg edges.

GIRL'S SWIMSUIT

Materials
50 cm cotton/lycra two-way
stretch fabric, 60 cm wide
220 cm swimsuit elastic, 1 cm wide
Small pieces of contrast cotton
knits for appliqué

Instructions
1 Cut one each of Front 21 and Back 22. 6 mm seams and 1 cm edges allowed.
2 Stitch left side seam. Press.
3 Prepare appliqué patches using the fish on this page and the starfish on page 74. Refer to Machine Appliqué Tips on page 74. Position on swimsuit from front to back across left side seam. Appliqué. Finish with machine embroidery as desired.
4 Stitch right side seam, shoulder seams and crutch seam. Press.
5 Cut elastic to fit snugly around neck edge. Join ends. Mark neck edge and elastic into quarters. Pin elastic evenly around wrong side of neck edge, matching markings. Stitch in place using zigzag to allow elasticised edge to stretch. Turn under 1 cm at neck edge, zigzag stitch to finish. Repeat for armhole and leg edges.

MACHINE APPLIQUE TIPS

The easiest method of appliqué also gives the most professional finish. It's a good idea to wash all your fabrics first to remove any dressing or finish. Assemble the fabric along with the design templates and some paper-backed fusible webbing. Transfer the designs onto the fabric, then cut out leaving 2 cm extra all round. Fuse fabric pieces to webbing, then cut out precisely around each piece of the design. The webbing makes the pieces easy to work with and also stops the edges from fraying. Peel off paper backing, carefully position pieces onto garment and then fuse. Stitch all around edges of design using a close zigzag (satin stitch), approximately 2.5 mm wide and 0.5 mm in stitch length. Once all pieces of a motif are applied in this way, you can stitch over them using a variety of stitches for more detail and interest. Machine and hand embroidery are equally effective. These starfish and fish appliqués are decorated with pieces of contrast fabric, zigzag and eyelet stitching. It is best to experiment and practise on scraps before appliquéing the actual garment. Press when finished.

T-SHIRT

Materials

- 50 cm cotton knit, 150 cm wide
- 10 cm ribbing, 90 cm wide
- Small pieces of contrast cotton knits for appliqué

Instructions

1 Cut one Front 13, one Back 14 and two Sleeves 15. Cut neck ribbing 6 cm x 29 cm (31 cm).

2 Prepare appliqué patches using big fish on page 75 and starfish on this page. Refer to Machine Appliqué Tips. Position as desired on t-shirt front. Appliqué. Finish with machine embroidery as desired.

3 Stitch shoulder seams. Press. Stitch sleeves to armholes, matching shoulder points. Press. Stitch front to back along underarm seams, matching underarm points. Press.

4 Stitch ends of neck ribbing together. Fold in half, seam inside. Pin evenly around neck edge with raw edges together and ribbing seam at centre back. Stitch with a zigzag or overlocking stitch to allow neck opening to stretch sufficiently. Press seam away from ribbing.

5 Turn under 1.5 cm and 1.5 cm again at hem. Topstitch and edgestitch to finish. Repeat for sleeve hems.

CROP TOP

Materials

- 40 cm cotton knit, 150 cm wide
- 10 cm ribbing, 90 cm wide
- Small pieces of contrasting cotton knits for appliqué

Instructions

1 Cut one Front 13, one Back 14 and two Sleeves 15. Cut neck ribbing 6 cm x 29 cm (31 cm).

2 Prepare appliqué patches using fish on page 75 and starfish on this page. Refer to Machine Appliqué Tips. . Position as desired on t-shirt front. Appliqué. Finish with machine embroidery as desired.

3 Stitch shoulder seams. Press. Stitch sleeves to armholes, matching shoulder points. Press. Stitch front to back along underarm seams, matching underarm points. Press.

4 Stitch ends of neck ribbing together. Fold in half, seam inside. Pin evenly around neck edge with raw edges together and ribbing seam at centre back. Stitch with a zigzag or overlocking stitch to allow neck opening to stretch sufficiently. Press seam away from ribbing.

5 Turn under 1.5 cm and 1.5 cm again at hem. Topstitch and edgestitch to finish. Repeat for sleeve hems.

SHORTS

Materials

- 40 cm cotton knit, 150 cm wide
- 50 cm elastic, 2 cm wide

Instructions

1 Cut two of Shorts Front & Back 18. Seam allowances are 1 cm, hem allowances 2 cm.

2 Stitch centre front and centre back seams. Press. Stitch along inside leg seam, matching crutch points. Press.

3 To form casing, turn under 4 cm at waist edge; stitch 3 cm from edge, leaving opening at centre back. Edgestitch close to top edge to neaten. Cut elastic to fit waist, insert and join ends. Stitch across opening.

4 Turn under 1 cm and 1 cm again at hems. Topstitch and edgestitch to finish.

PIRATE PANTS

Materials

- 60 cm cotton knit, 150 cm wide
- 50 cm elastic, 2 cm wide

Instructions

1 Cut two of Shorts Front & Back 18. Seam allowances are 1 cm, hem allowances 2 cm.

2 Stitch centre front and centre back seams. Press. Stitch along inside leg seam, matching crutch points. Press.

3 To form casing, turn under 4 cm at waist edge; stitch 3 cm from edge, leaving opening at centre back. Edgestitch close to top edge to neaten. Cut elastic to fit waist, insert and join ends. Stitch across opening.

4 Turn under 1 cm and 1 cm again at hems. Topstitch and edgestitch to finish.

TRACK PANTS

Materials

40 cm cotton knit, 150 cm wide
Small pieces of contrast cotton
   knits for appliqué
50 cm elastic, 2 cm wide

Instructions

1 Cut two of Shorts Front & Back 18. Seam allowances are 1 cm, hem allowances 2 cm.

2 Prepare appliqué patches using small fish on page 73 and fish big on this page, referring to Machine Appliqué Tips. Position as desired on left leg. Appliqué. Finish with machine embroidery as desired.

3 Cut two of Shorts Front & Back 18. Seam allowances are 1 cm, hem allowances 2 cm.

4 Stitch centre front and centre back seams. Press. Stitch along inside leg seam, matching crutch points. Press.

5 To form casing, turn under 4 cm at waist edge; stitch 3 cm from edge, leaving opening at centre back. Edgestitch close to top edge to neaten. Cut elastic to fit waist, insert and join ends. Stitch across opening.

6 Turn under 1 cm and 1 cm again at hems. Topstitch and edgestitch to finish.

HOODED TRACK TOP

Materials

50 cm cotton knit, 150 cm wide
10 cm ribbing, 90 cm wide
Small pieces of contrasting cotton
   knits for appliqué

Instructions

1 Cut one Front 13, one Back 14, two Sleeves 15, two Hoods 16 and one Pocket 17. Cut neck ribbing 6 cm x 29 cm (31 cm) and two pieces of pocket ribbing 6 cm x 15 cm.

2 Prepare appliqué patches using small fish page 73 and big fish on this page. Refer to Machine Appliqué Tips.

Position as desired on pocket. Appliqué. Finish with machine embroidery as desired.

3 Fold pocket ribbing pieces in half lengthways. Stitch to curved edges of pocket. Press seams away from ribbing. Turn under 1 cm at top of pocket. Press. Pin pocket to front, matching raw edges at sides and hem. Baste. Edgestitch top of pocket to front.

4 Stitch shoulder seams. Press. Stitch sleeves to armholes, matching shoulder points. Press. Stitch front to back along underarm seams, matching underarm points and including pocket sides in seam. Press.

5 Stitch curved centre seam of hood.

Press. Turn under 1.5 cm then 1.5 cm again along front edge of hood. Edgestitch and topstitch to finish. Pin hood to neck edge, matching centre backs and fronts. Baste.

6 Stitch ends of neck ribbing together. Fold in half, seam inside. Pin evenly around neck edge, over hood, with raw edges together and ribbing seam at centre back. Stitch through all layers with a zigzag or overlocking stitch to allow neck opening to stretch sufficiently. Press seam away from ribbing.

7 Turn under 1.5 cm and 1.5 cm again at hem, including pocket at front. Topstitch and edgestitch to finish. Repeat for sleeve hems.

FISH AND STARFISH KNIT TOP

See measurements for different sizes on page 47.

Materials

Thorobred's 4Ply Crochet and Knitting Cotton (50g) Balls:

Size		2	3	4
(Mid Blue)	MC	2	3	3
(Coral)	C1	1	1	1
(Pond Green)	C2	1	1	1
(Yellow)	C3	1	1	1

1 pair 2.75 mm (No.12) knitting needles
1 pair 3.25 mm (No.10) knitting needles
2 stitch holders
Tapestry needle for embroidery
Size 2 only - 3 buttons.

Instructions

TENSION:

28 sts to 10 cm over st st, using 3.25 mm needles.

BACK:

Using 2.75 mm needles and MC, cast on 81 (91, 99) sts.

1st Row: (wrong side) Knit.

Rep 1st row until band measures 2.5 (3, 3) cm from beg, working last row on wrong side.

Change to 3.25 mm needles. **

Work 90 (98, 114) rows in st st (1 row K, 1 row P).

SHAPE SHOULDERS:

Cast off 13 (15, 17) sts at beg of next 4 rows.

Leave rem 29 (31, 31) sts on a stitch holder .

FRONT:

Work as for Back to **.

Work rows 1 to 68 (74, 88) inclusive from Graph, using Bobbin method.

SHAPE NECK:

Next Row: (right side) K31 (35, 39), turn.

*** Dec one st at neck edge in foll alt rows 5 times. 26 (30, 34) sts.

Work 3 (13, 15) rows. ***

NOTE: This side of neck is 8 rows shorter than other side to accommodate shoulder bands for 1st size only.

SHAPE SHOULDER:

Cast off 13 (15, 17) sts at beg of next row.

Work 1 row. Cast off.

Slip next 19 (21, 21) sts at centre front onto a stitch holder and leave. With right side facing, join yarn to rem sts and patt to end.

Keeping graph correct, work from *** to ***.

Work 9 (1, 1) row/s.

SHAPE SHOULDER:

Work as for other side.

SLEEVES:

Using 2.75 mm needles and MC, cast on 67 (75, 81) sts.

1st Row: (wrong side) Knit.

Rep 1st row until band measures 2.5 cm from beg, working last row on wrong side.

Change to 3.25 mm needles.

Work 10 (12, 14) rows in st st.

SHAPE TOP:

Cast off 7 (7, 8) sts at beg of next 6 rows. Cast off rem sts.

NECKBAND:

Using back stitch, join right shoulder seam. With right side facing, using 2.75 mm needles and MC, beg at front left shoulder, knit up 75 (89, 92) sts evenly around neck edge (including sts from stitch holders).

1st Row: Knit.

Rep 1st row 8 times more.

Cast off.

Size 2 only:

FRONT SHOULDER BAND:

With right side facing, using 2.75 mm needles and MC, knit up 29 sts evenly along front left shoulder and Neckband.

1st Row: Knit.

Rep 1st row twice more.

Next Row: K6, (cast off 2 sts, K7) twice, cast off 2 sts, K3.

Next Row: K3, cast on 2 sts, (K7, cast on 2 sts) twice,K6.

Knit 4 rows. Cast off.

BACK SHOULDER BAND:

Work as for Front Shoulder band, omitting buttonholes. Place Front Shoulder Band over Back Shoulder Band and catch together at armhole edge.

Size 3 and 4 only:

Using back stitch, join left shoulder and Neckband seam.

To make up for all sizes:

Using stem stitch (or back stitch) and C3, work details on Fish and Star Fish indicated by dark lines on Graph. Using back stitch, sew in sleeves (armhole depth 11.5 (13, 14) cm), then join side and sleeve seams. Sew on buttons for size 2.

FISH AND STARFISH KNIT CHART

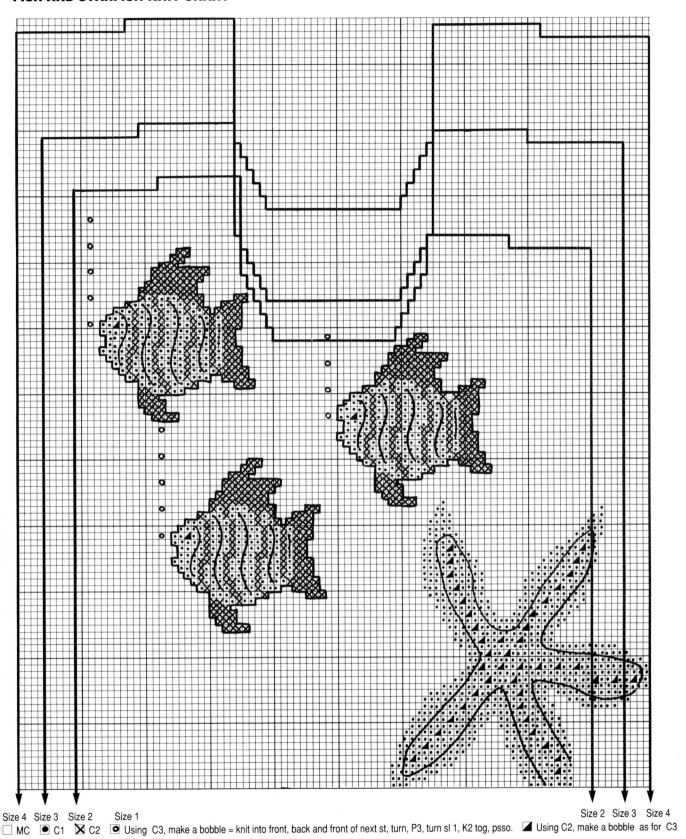

Size 4   Size 3   Size 2   Size 1

Size 2   Size 3   Size 4

☐ MC   ⊙ C1   ✕ C2   ⊚ Using C3, make a bobble = knit into front, back and front of next st, turn, P3, turn sl 1, K2 tog, psso.   ◣ Using C2, make a bobble as for C3

Stockists

Following is a list of retailers whose products appear in this publication, as well as manufacturers/distributors of other items who can be contacted for details of local stockists. We gratefully acknowledge the particular assistance given by Hill Textiles and Ray Toby in the preparation of this book.

Bonza Brats
713 Military Road
Mosman NSW 2088
Ph: (02) 969 6565

Brosalco
23 Royalston Street
Paddington NSW 2021
Ph: (02) 361 6249

Cancer Council of NSW
153 Dowling Street
Woolloomooloo NSW 2011
Ph: (02) 334 1900

DMC Needlecraft
55 Carrington Street
Marrickville NSW 2204
Ph: (02) 559 3088

Framing Corner
228a Chatswood Chase
345 Victoria Avenue
Chatswood NSW 2067
Ph: (02) 412 1969

Grace Brothers
Victor Street
Chatswood NSW 2067
Ph: (02) 412 0111

Hansa Toys
8 Bridge Street
Granville NSW 2142
Ph: (02) 682 1466

Hartland Fashion Agencies
45 Market Street
Sydney NSW 2000
Ph: (02) 267 7043

Hide 'n' Seek
611 Military Road
Mosman NSW 2088
Ph: (02) 960 1039

Hill Textiles
81 Carnavon Street
Auburn NSW 2144
Ph: (02) 648 5888

Lincraft
Gallery Level
Imperial Arcade
Sydney NSW 2000
Ph: (02) 221 5111

McCalls Patterns
18 Newton Street
Alexandria NSW 2015
Ph: (02) 550 1044

Myart
55 Carrington Street
Marrickville NSW 2204
Ph: (02) 559 3088

Ray Toby
17 Ralph Street
Alexandria NSW 2015
Ph: (02) 693 5000

Sweet Violets
773 Military Road
Mosman NSW 2088
Ph: (02) 969 9381

Task Lighting
16 Alex Pike Drive
Raleigh NSW 2454
Ph: (066) 55 5155

Teddy & Friends
2a Waverley Street
Bondi Junction NSW 2022
Ph: (02) 369 4709

124a Chatswood Chase
345 Victoria Avenue
Chatswood NSW 2067
Ph: (02) 413 1780

Head office ph: (02) 660 3577

The Body Shop
Head Office
57 Railway Parade
Marrickville NSW 2204
Ph: (02) 517 1300

The Teddy Bear Shop
162 Military Road
Neutral Bay NSW 2089
Ph: (02) 953 3394

Make a handy envelope for your pattern pieces – cut out top semicircle
along dotted line, then stick the right hand side and bottom
of this page to the back cover with sticky tape.